THE CULCHIE'S GUIDE TO DUBLIN

THE CULCHIE'S GUIDE TO DUBLIN

JIM CONNOLLY

MERCIER PRESS
IRISH PUBLISHER – IRISH STORY

MERCIER PRESS

Cork

www.mercierpress.ie

Trade enquiries to CMD BookSource,
55a Spruce Avenue, Stillorgan Industrial Park,
Blackrock, County Dublin

ISBN: 978 1 85635 635 0

10 9 8 7 6 5 4 3 2 1

A CIP record for this title is available from the British Library

Printed and bound in the EU.

CONTENTS

To me Jackeen missus (the biggest Malahide in Dalkey)
and me tree chislers

INTRODUCTION

Ah the Big Smoke – spiritual home of Guinness, about a million Dubs and you, I'm guessing.

Fear not – everything you need to know about Dublin and Dubliners is in here: what sights to see; where to eat and drink; what areas to avoid at all costs; where to pick up a nurse or a guard; how to follow a Dub's directions; and, of course, where to find the ultimate pint of Guinness.

Few things are certainties in life but this is one – if you read the whole of this book you'll know more about Dublin than most Dubs – *no kiddin der bud*. You see Dubs actually know very little about Dublin, largely because they tend to stay local. For example, you'll never find a core southsider visiting Raheny. But Dubs wouldn't be aware of all that Raheny has to offer – it's where Bono got hitched for example (before fast tracking southside to join the rest of the A-listers in Dalkey).

And Dublin isn't the only thing that Dubs don't know about: they don't know why they're called Jackeens, they don't know anything about Molly Malone and they know even less about the truth behind their hurling achievements.

But we know and it's all here. This is the ultimate, no

nonsense, humour packed, timesaving, politically incorrect and downright brilliant introduction to Dublin's fair city.

CHAPTER 1

THE MOST HONEST MAP OF DUBLIN, EVER

There are a few maps included in this guide, but none are as honest as this one. In fact we'd go so far as to say that this is the most honest map of Dublin ever, not only in the history of printing but in history, full stop.

You see, this map tells you how desirable it is to live, rent or socialise in all parts of Dublin. It doesn't come any more politically incorrect or blunt than this.

It almost seems obvious that every city should have a map such as this so that visitors from all walks can quickly identify the places that they should avoid at all costs. In fact it's bordering on shameful that the government doesn't produce the map for you. The gardaí know exactly where the no-go areas of the city are – we should insist that they are clearly sign-posted with 18-certificates so that the rest of us can give them a wide berth.

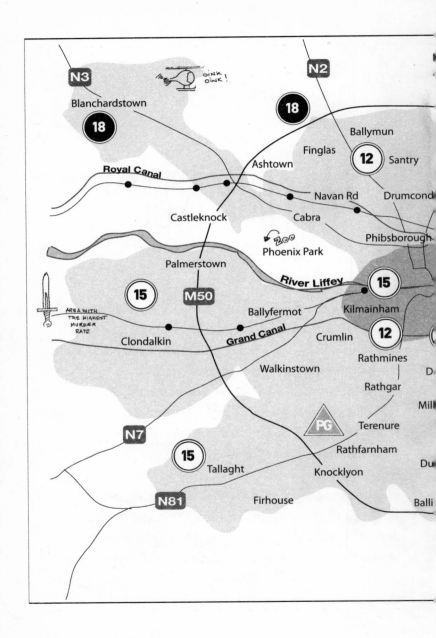

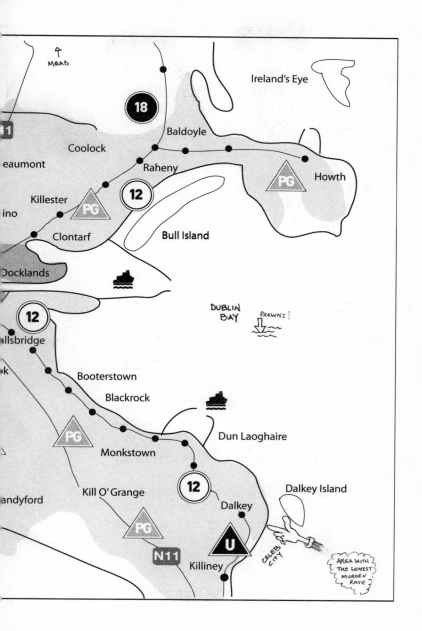

MEAD

Ireland's Eye

18

Baldoyle

Coolock

eaumont

Raheny

PG Howth

Killester

PG

12

ino

Clontarf

Bull Island

Docklands

DUBLIN
BAY

PRAWNS!

12

llsbridge

k

Booterstown

Blackrock

PG

Dun Laoghaire

Monkstown

Kill O' Grange

12

Dalkey Island

andyford

Dalkey

PG

U

CELEB
CITY

N11

AREA WITH
THE LOWEST
MURDER
RATE

Killiney

In fact all areas of Dublin should have public information signs on the boundaries so that you know whether you should wear your overcoat or flak jacket when visiting, e.g. 'You're now entering Ballywherever – scene of 450 car thefts and 29 assaults in the last year'.

And before you use your ladder to climb up on the horse, we know that the majority of people living in these areas are salt of the earth, wouldn't harm a fly, do anything for you types of Dubs. We love them; we just hate their neighbours.

So in the interests of truth, here it is:

Certificate	Description
U	The safest and most desirable location you can get. If you parked your car there overnight there is a 100% chance of it being there the next day. Businesses don't use metal shutters, owners clean up after their dogs and there's probably a Bang and Olufsen store within walking distance.

Certificate	Description
PG	Still a very safe area. It's likely that the residents have successfully fought council plans for the placement of halting sites in the area numerous times. There are council estates in the area but they're mature and the market for them is buoyant. Guards usually only come out to tell you to turn down the music but the Criminal Assets Bureau are kept busy with the white collar crime. Sometime in the past decade the local pub won Black and White pub of the year (and still has the plaque to prove it).
12	Mature suburbs of Dublin that have sprawled in recent years as the green field sites have been built on by developers who managed to fit amazing numbers of houses into minute sites. Alleyways are covered in graffiti – all of which is spelled properly. All businesses use metal shutters. The local pub has a bar area where the locals stare if you go in.
15	Characterised by the amount of council housing – there's loads of it. The rest of the area is fairly decent and is largely made up of big estates built on controversially rezoned areas. No one takes the shortcut through the field after dark. Most teens know how much an ounce of Black Moroccan costs. There are vans and lorries parked outside many of the houses. The smoking area of the pub is jammed.

18

Regularly featured in the news usually for drug or gangland related crime. Firemen frequently end up in ambulances after call-outs. There are piebald ponies in most green spaces. Unemployment is high, as are most of the people in the dole office queue. The garda helicopter is a frequent visitor. Truancy rates are high and joy-riding is rife.

And how did we arrive at this inspired depiction of the rare auld town? Well, as with all best ideas, the test in this case was simple. We looked at various criteria for each area which included:

How many celebrities live in the area?

Looking at the numbers of celebrities in the area is a simple test to establish how desirable the area is – if it is good enough for Boyzone, then it can't be that bad. However, it's important to note that we were really looking for the A-list celebrities, as opposed to *Crimewatch* celebrities. So, whilst Rathcoole may be where many of our successful criminal celebrities live, no points were awarded.

Would a guard choose to live there?

We initially looked at garda numbers for each area but surprisingly, these don't always correlate to crime. For instance, Donnybrook is heavily populated with gardaí but a lot of their daily activities are taken up with false alarms (literally).

So we decided to interview ex-guards and ask them to tell us the likelihood of them living in various parts of the city, given their familiarity with them.

What is the murder rate for the area?

For the purpose of collating these statistics, the Central Statistics Office breaks Dublin into metropolitan areas. Southsiders will be disappointed to hear that the most likely place to be murdered is the southern region (Tallaght and surrounding areas). However Southsiders can take solace in the fact that the safest part is the eastern region (Dun Laoghaire to Bray).

Others

We also looked at each area under the headings of:

- average house prices
- school rankings
- unemployment statistics

Finally, we carried out Google searches using numerous search criteria such as 'dangerous Dublin' and 'safe Dublin'.

Conclusion

If you're looking to rent – use the map. If you're wondering whether to get the bus or a taxi home – use the map. And most importantly, if you're being hit on by a complete stranger, find out where they live – you can use the map to see if it's safer to go to your place or theirs.

For convenience we've set out a complete quick reference A-Z guide below.

	Certificate
Ballyfermot	18
Ballymun	15
Blackrock	PG
Blanchards-town	18
Bray	PG
Bridewell	15
Cabinteely	PG
Cabra	PG
Clondalkin	15
Clontarf	PG

	Certificate
Coolock	18
Crumlin	15
Dalkey	U
Donnybrook	PG
Dundrum	PG
Dun Laoghaire	12
Enniskerry	PG
Finglas	18
Fitzgibbon St	15
Greystones	PG

	Certificate
Harcourt Terrace	PG
Howth	PG
Irishtown	12
Kevin Street	15
Kill-o-the-Grange	PG
Kilmainham	15
Leixlip	12
Lucan	12
Lusk	12
Malahide	PG
Mountjoy	15
Pearse Street	12
Raheny	12
Rathcoole	12

	Certificate
Rathfarnham	12
Rathmines	12
Ronanstown	18
Rush	PG
Santry	12
Shankill	12
Skerries	PG
Stepaside	PG
Store Street	15
Sundrive Road	15
Swords	12
Tallaght	15
Terenure	PG
Whitehall	12

CHAPTER 2

YOU AND THEM: DUBLIN'S CULTURAL DIFFERENCES

While Dublin's gone all European, Dubliners haven't. They still refer to four populations of inhabitant:

Northsiders
Southsiders
Blow-Ins (culchies)
Foreigners (everyone else)

Northsiders

What constitutes a northsider? Well that absolutely depends on who you ask. Hard-core southsiders consider anyone with a Dublin accent to be a northsider (seriously). There are other areas on the southside that

even southsiders themselves disown and deem northside – Clondalkin for example.

The correct position of course is that the northside of the city lies on the north side of the Liffey. And to make life even easier An Post has simplified the divide by allocating even postal codes to the south and odd to the north. Dublin 2, 4, 6 … all southside and 1, 3, 5, … northside.

The exception to the odd/even rule is of course the president of Ireland because Áras an Uachtaráin has been given the honorary southside address of Dublin 8. This little nugget will secure an extra point for you at your next Dublin pub quiz.

While the southside has its fair share of undesirable areas, the northside wins the dodgy territory contest hands down. This is best captured by the urban legend of the tourist that asks a local in Sheriff Street if his car would be there when he got back. He was told in reply, 'mista, yew cud paark yer car anywhere in the bleedin' city and it'll be here when ya get back'.

Similar to their southside counterparts, northsiders are fairly easy to spot. D'accent is a far'ly obviees characteristic, but in case you're out of earshot there are a number of giveaways that you can rely on:

- Lads with a blade 1 haircut on the back and sides and a blond dollop on top
- Girls with mullets
- Anyone driving a car with the word 'turbo' pasted on the back window
- Blokes with 'made in Mountjoy' tattoos
- Blokes with mobile phones attached to their belts
- Blokes who walk on the balls of their feet whilst swinging their shoulders
- Anyone ordering a Fat Frog at the bar
- Blokes with gold chains on display outside of their clothes
- Anyone wearing a Dubs jersey

All joking aside, northsiders aren't in anyway near as hung

up about the northside/southside divide as southsiders and therefore they tend to be somewhat more genuine and earthy. They are also more likely to be involved in the Dublin GAA scene so culchies have marginally more in common with them. However, this is not always a good thing because the Dublin fans can be a little intimidating on match days – after stuffing them on home territory anyone from Meath, Tyrone and Kerry will know what we mean.

Southsiders

The first thing to know about southsiders is that there are two types – those that simply live in the southside and those that live in the southside but want you to know it – snobs.

To the southside snob anyone who speaks with a Dublin accent is considered to be a northsider irrespective of where they live. Spotting the snob variety is simple. If you manage to hear them loike you know, it's soooo obvious, it's as clear as Bluetooth signal in the beemer loike you know.

However, if you can't hear them speak then the visuals are just as easy to spot. They are numerous but here are a few:

- Girls driving current Mini Cooper models – girls driving two- or three-year-old models are wannabees

- Girls with tans that look real. These chicks have been well bred and know to wash their hands after applying the fake tan thus leaving their hands naturally white. Any bird with umpa-lumpa hands ain't no southsider snob – no way girlfriend
- Blokes with tans and white hands
- Blokes who look like they paid someone to dye their hair
- Blokes without earrings
- Blokes driving expensive cars with stickers that say 'my other car's a Porsche' – these bastards are not lying, they're simply rubbing it in
- Blokes who persistently look at the time – they're really checking to make sure you've noticed that it's the same wristwatch that Beckham used in the Boss ad
- Blokes or girls who have no idea of any bus route other than the 46A
- Blokes or girls wearing Leinster shirts

Southsiders also have a calculated logic as to why the southside is better than the north. They'll quote you absurd yet irrefutable evidence to support these hypotheses. For example, every single international embassy is on the southside but every prison is on the northside including Wheatfield because loike, jeez who in their right mind considers Dublin 22 as being really southside?

And when it comes to tourist attractions southsiders

will draw your attention to the wealth of culturally abundant attractions in Dublin 2 – Trinity, the old parliament buildings at Bank of Ireland, the Café en Seine – compared with the military and criminal attractions on the other side of the river – the Four Courts and Collins Barracks.

Listen to them long enough and they actually start to make sense, actually, oops, it's starting …

Blow-ins (Non Dublin-based Irish)

Not that it'll be news, but you go under the collective names of boggers, muckers, mulchies, culchies, rednecks,

ruralites, sheep-shaggers, muck savages and country bumpkins.

It is important to note that, to Dubs, culchie is a term that applies to anyone not from Dublin. So, people from Bray, Celbridge and the like are as culchie as the culchiest culchie in culchieland.

There are so many cultural differences between Dubs and culchies that we've devoted an entire chapter to the issue and called it the Culchie Survival Guide – Chapter 7.

Foreigners

Foreigners fall into two Dublin categories – tourists (foreigners) and non-national residents (bloody foreigners).

The non-Irish community in Dublin has exploded over the past few years. Out of the 195 independent states in the world, we actually have representatives from 188 living in Ireland and the largest concentration is in Dublin.

The top five nationalities living here are British, Polish, Lithuanian, Nigerian and Latvian.

Dubs have a sort of love-hate relationship with foreigners, the root of which lies with the cultural differences between them:

Work ethic

Some nationalities work too hard and show us up (try

keeping up with an Eastern European builder for a day) whereas other nationalities don't seem to work at all.

Language Barrier

Dubs have all the time in the world to teach you English if you meet them in a bar:

> Typical Dublin girl chatting up a foreign bloke:
> 'Ooohhh I love your accent, where are you from, you big hunky man.'

> Typical Dublin bloke chatting up a foreign girl:
> 'Great legs señora, what time do they open?'

However, Dubs have zero patience when language is a barrier in a business situation – when ordering Munchies and getting a Crunchie for example.

Frankness

We (the Irish we) are not very honest when honesty would result in impoliteness. Some foreigners suffer from the same trait (e.g. Scots and Australians), but most don't. If they think your arse looks big in that dress, they'll tell you. We think they're rude because we'd never be so honest (or brave).

Generosity

This manifests itself mainly at the bar. We (again the Irish we) like to buy rounds of drinks, but expect a decent return for the investment. While the English, Australian and numerous other nationalities embrace this practice, others don't. (Not pointing any fingers there Hamish.)

CHAPTER 3

THINGS DUBS SHOULD KNOW BUT DON'T, LIKE ...

... what is a Jackeen?

There is an amazing lack of knowledge on this front. Perhaps it's regression or maybe it's embarrassment, but the reason Dubs are called Jacks or Jackeens is simply because the Dubs of the early nineteenth century were in fact quite supportive of their British landlords. Who would've thought?

Waving Union Jack flags would have been common practice whenever a royal came to visit. Jackeen was coined from the Jack part of the British flag coupled with the Irish for little – pronounced een – Little Brit in other words.

It's not clear when exactly the name was first used. Jackeen does appear in Webster's dictionary in 1913 with an unrelated definition so perhaps it wasn't until the 1916 Rising that the name stuck to Dubs.

Dublin society at the time of the Rising was initially against the activities of the Republican boys in the GPO and Union Jacks were supposedly flown outside many Dublin homes at the time. It wasn't until the British began executing the lads that public opinion took a huge swing, by which time it was too late – Dubs were now Jackeens.

... why they call culchies, culchies?

I presume being called a culchie by a Jackeen would be marginally more stomachable if Dubs actually knew where the tag came from.

Mind you it's debateable where the word culchie comes from in the first place. You can break the phonetics up into *cul* and *tí* to get the Irish for back of the house, but this makes no sense.

Some believe that it's the anglicised version of *coilte-mach* (the Irish for Kiltimagh in Mayo), which translates roughly as 'out in the woods' or in a Dubs head – from the woods – and makes a little more sense.

But the clever money is on the fact that the most likely source of culchie is from a shortened version of agriculture, as in agricultural science. This degree was introduced to the syllabus at UCD in the 1960s and all of the students taking it were nicknamed cult-ies, which then became culchies, which then became synonymous with anyone not from Dublin.

... what are the areas of Dublin ending in 'O'?

Possibly the most common question to appear in a Dublin pub quiz is 'name the five areas of Dublin that end in the letter "O"?'

The ones that don't count are:

Monto	just because it appears in a Dubliners' song doesn't negate the fact that it's actually short for Montgomery Lane
Sorrento	may be a lovely Terrace in Dalkey but it doesn't qualify as an area of Dublin
Phibsboro'	Phibsborough, ya plank (as they say in Dublin)
Vico	another lovely Dalkey road, but that's all
Martello	where exactly is this supposed to be?

The correct five are in fact:

Pimlico	yes there's one in Ireland too
Rialto	built on an abandoned part of the Grand Canal and has since been abandoned by anyone who can afford to live anywhere nicer
Marino	the name conjures up images of Monte Carlo, but you'll be sorely disappointed in the sightseeing if you ever go there
Portabello	means 'beautiful door' in Italian and 'student city' in Dublin
Dublin Zoo	don't blame the messenger, this is the fifth one

... anything about Molly Malone

True Dublin wit would dictate that Dubs know loads about Molly Malone – she lived in Dublin, she smelled of fish, she owned a wheelbarrow, she was forever crying alive-alive-o, she died of a high temperature and now haunts the city. Yeah that and that her real name is the Tart with the Cart. Well done Dubs.

But apart from the lyrics to the song (which by the way is called 'Cockles and Mussels', not 'Dublin's Fair City') Dubs know very little about the Trollope with the Scallops.

So wha' d'story den? Brace yourselves because I've

some bad news for you. A full account of the Dish with the Fish is set out on pages 55–57, but the abridged version is that Molly Malone never existed at all. Molly Malone is an urban myth fuelled by sloppy research and a dodgy statue commissioned to commemorate the city's millennium. Ask yourself this, if Molly Malone wheeled a wheelbarrow then why is her statue wheeling a handcart (one with two wheels and not one)?

And to make matters worse there's no evidence that the song was even written by a Dub or even an Irishman – apparently that honour goes to a Scot who could have easily attributed it to London, Cork or Belfast's fair city.

Perhaps the song does have some basis in truth but unfortunately the details that are currently attributed to her legend are more cock 'n' bull than cockles and mussels!

... what and where is the Pale?

This really surprised me but many Dubs really don't have a clue about the Pale – what it was, where it was and where it came from. Most people from beyond the Pale know a little more, but just in case you're a Dub trying to learn a little about your own heritage, the Pale refers to an area of land that was subject to British influence. At its peak the Pale would have stretched as far north as Dundalk and as far south as Waterford. But as the Irish gradually fought back over the ages (Norman times to Tudor times) the Pale was eventually reduced to a twenty-mile radius around Dublin. Those inside the Pale were the ancestors to the current Jackeens and those outside represent those with a culchie heritage.

In the interests of thoroughness we should point out that the word Pale means a boundary so when we refer to the Pale we're really talking about the Dublin Pale.

... how to speak a *cúpla focail*

Tá brón orm an rud céanna a rá mar gheall ar gach éinne ach ó thaobh ar ár dteanga náisiúnta de, níl daoine ó Áth Cliath ró-chliste. Chun é seo a chruthú tá sé scriofa anseoi nGaeilge símplí. Nílmid ag súil le h-aon ghearán ach má tá gearán agat seol email chugainn.

www.imadubwhocanactuallyspeakirish.com

... why is Hill 16 called Hill 16?

In fairness (as they say in Dublin) most Dublin GAA heads probably have an inkling as to how Hill 16 got its name but they'd still go 50:50 or phone a friend if you asked them to put any money on it.

You see there are two schools of thought as to where the name came from. The first is that Hill 16 got its name from the 16 people killed at Croke Park on Bloody Sunday, November 1921. This is wrong because only 14 people were killed in Croke Park itself.

Others believe that the hill got its name because it was built from the rubble of the city after the 1916 Rising. There may, however, be some truth to this. Croke Park always had a hill and it was originally called Hill 60. This name was given to the hill as a mark of respect to the Allied soldiers who died at the original Hill 60 in Ypres, Belgium during the First World War.

Although unsubstantiated (anywhere) there is a claim that Hill 60 got bigger when some of the rubble taken from the city after the 1916 Rising was dumped there. Hill 16 was adopted as the new and more patriotic name for the hill.

And if you do need to phone a friend, phone Phil Archibald in the GAA Museum at Croke Park.

...how to make Dublin Coddle

Dublin Coddle is a sausage and bacon stew, favoured by Dubs because it's cheap to make. Not only do Dubliners not know how to make Coddle, they actually don't know how to cook, period. This is simply because Dubs don't leave home until late in life. Whereas the rest of the country have to leave home to go college or work, Dubs don't: there are plenty of employers and colleges on their doorstep so they tend to stay at home longer and therefore don't develop any survival skills such as cooking.

In light of this we're setting out a recipe for Coddle written in a Dublin-friendly manner.

Ingredients

How much	Of what	Where to find them
4 tennis-ball sized	Potatoes	On the stage after a Coldplay concert
1 clove	Garlic	In the same aisle as the silver bullets, wooden stakes and other vampire-repelling stuff
1 lb	Pork sausages	Avoid the temptation to buy the cheapest pack on the shelf and go to your butcher for some decent ones
1 lb	Rashers	While in the butchers pick these up too
2 large	Carrots	In the vegetable aisle and probably stacked in alphabetical order between the bananas and the dates

2 medium	Onions	Some elderly neighbours back garden
2	Vegetable stock cubes	Try your neighbours press
Some	Mixed herbs	In one of those Schwarz jars that has been taking up space in your press for decades

The Recipe

What you're aiming for here is a stew where everything ends up in the same pot, so have one ready.

1. Start by browning the sausages – this means frying them in a frying pan long enough for them to change colour. You're not actually cooking them at this point so as soon as they look nice, toss them into the big stew pot. If you're completely devoid of cooking experience you should carry out this exercise on a medium heat, i.e. if your cooker has 5 notches, stick it to number 3.
2. Do the same with the rashers.
3. Chop up the onions and garlic and fry them for a couple of minutes in the same pan and toss them into the pot along with the sausages and rashers.
4. Now, this may sound gross but it's all about flavour

– pour water into the now dirty frying pan and get all the crusty bits off the bottom and pour this juice into the stewing pot.

5.   Peel the carrots and spuds, roughly chop them and add them to the stew pot.

6.   Crumble the stock cubes over the contents and fill the pot with just enough water so that everything is submerged. Add a teaspoon of mixed herbs.

7.   Bring it to the boil and once it starts to bubble turn your cooker down to notch 1 on the 5-notch scale (this will maintain the stew at a simmer). Walk away and come back in an hour and a half. That's it.

... where things are in Dublin?

Admittedly Dublin is a big city, but you'd think that if you'd lived there for your entire life, you'd know where things are. Try asking a Dub where the Natural History Museum is for example and they'll stare blankly back at you. And when they do know where something is they're incapable of giving meaningful directions because the other thing that Dubs don't know is street names. They tend to give directions by reference to the pubs that you'll pass to get to wherever you're going.

So, if by chance you asked for directions outside, say, the Mansion House and the Dub did know where the Natural History museum was, then the directions would be something like ...

Roit ... go up der ri past the Dawson and hang a lef
rown d'corner and keep goin past the Shelbourne and
O'Donogues 'n den han' a leff after Foleys roit, and it's roit
there on the leff.

Here's a handy guide to help you decipher in general
what's being said:

If a Dub says:	*They mean:*
O'Donoghues	Merrion Row
The Shelbourne	St Stephen's Green
The Dawson	Dawson Street
Foleys	Merrion Row

CHAPTER 4

THE OTHER 31 COUNTIES IN THE ORDER THAT DUBS HATE YOU THE MOST

I think that it's more or less a certainty that most culchies would rank Dublin as the county they hate most. Why? It's too big, too fast, too full of traffic, people are rude, prices are high, service is crap, the accent is annoying, the locals are arrogant, superior and condescending, and they beat most other counties in football.

But on the flip side, what do Dubs think about the rest of the country? Although it seems like an obvious survey, up until now no one has bothered to establish who Dubs hate most and why.

So, for the first time ever here is the definitive list of counties presented in order that Dubs hate you the most:

Rank	County	Comments
1	Louth	Not even Andrea Corr could compensate for the two problems that Dubs have with 'Loud' – that poxy bleedin' accent and Dundalk.
2	Limerick	'The crime capital of Ireland, what a hole. The misery of *Angela's Ashes* 24/7, 365 – should be twinned with Calcutta', in one participant's words.
3	Meath	A lot of protest voting here – Dubs marking their territory. Many of the satellite towns such as Dunshaughlin are classifying themselves as Jackeens, and Jackeens are none too pleased. Apart from this Meath beats Dublin in football too often.
4	Offaly	Although Barack Obama's lineage is traceable to Offaly, so is Brian Cowan's.
5	Leitrim	There was confusion amongst our sample population as to whether Leitrim is a county or

Rank	County	Comments
		simply an annex of Sligo. On the positive side Leitrim was praised for being one of the only counties to still sell Sam Spudz crisps and Cadet red lemonade.
6	Laois	I think most thought they were voting for Portlaois (that some thought was a county), which holds bad traffic jam memories for most Dubs.
7	Carlow	There were only two southern (RoI) counties that received no positive comments. Unfortunately for Carlow, one of them was Carlow.
8	Tipperary	'It's where every young guard gets their anti-Dub attitude … it may be a long way [to Tipperary] but not half far enough', according to one person surveyed.
9	Westmeath	There were a whole bunch of
10	Longford	counties that fell into the
11	Monaghan	'midlands' category that Dubs

Rank	County	Comments
12	Cavan	have never been to nor want to
13	Kildare	go to. The midlands counties
14	Roscommon	lower down the list (and therefore more liked) were counties with better bypasses. Ouch.
15	Sligo	There was a marked decrease in negative comments between Roscommon and Sligo but it still surprised us that Sligo wasn't closer to the bottom of the list.
16	Armagh	The first of the counties to hit the 'Dubs are completely indifferent towards you' category.
17	Fermanagh	The second county to hit the 'indifferent' category.
18	Tyrone	The survey was conducted at an emotional time for Dubs in late August 2008, just days after the 3-14 to 1-8 football drumming – needless to say all of the feedback reflected this. We

Rank	County	Comments
		estimate that you'd have secured 22nd spot if you'd had the courtesy to lose the match.
19	Down	Down is the county that elicited the least amount of commentary – either positive or negative – thus making it the county that Dubs have virtually no opinion on.
20	Derry	The fifth in the 'indifferent' category.
21	Antrim	10 per cent of our survey had an opinion on Antrim, making you the northern county that generated the most commentary. 5 per cent loved you and 5 per cent didn't like you at all.
22	Kilkenny	The first county to score more positive than negative comments. A lot of stag and hen related memories here.
23	Waterford	Dubliners' ninth most favourite county. Most tended to prefer County Waterford to the city

Rank	County	Comments
		itself.
24	Clare	Beautiful county according to most comments (obviously they've forgotten about the Burren).
25	Cork	The county that split the population – got more positive votes than Kerry but also got the fourth most negative volume of comments – see 'Spilt Decision' below.
26	Mayo	The county where everybody's parents seemed to be from.
27	Wexford	Favourite holiday destination for Dubs. If a Dub owns a second home the likelihood is that it's in the sunny south-east.
28	Donegal	It appears the Dubs have never had a bad holiday in Donegal and most cited the landscape as their favourite bit.
29	Wicklow	The place many Dubs go to play golf, take the kids for a drive, have their wedding

Rank	County	Comments
		receptions and go for a swim (Brittas Bay).
30	Kerry	Fortunately for Kerry, far more Dubs love Kerry the place than hate Kerry the team.
31	Galway	Winner by a country mile. Simply the best county in the country according to Dubs, most of whom cited alcohol as the main driver for the vote. That and a non-threatening football team!

There are a few observations that warrant comment.

County Belfast

There is a small population of Dubs that think that Belfast, Dundalk and Portlaoise are all counties – 4 per cent of our sample population to be precise. These weren't new arrivals at Dublin airport, these were *bona fide* Dubs.

Sporting Rivalry

The Dubs that held the most robust opinions were those from a GAA background. These Dubs typically hated Kerry, Meath and Tyrone – for obvious reasons – but liked counties like Leitrim (for winning the Connacht championship in 1994 thus providing Dublin with a handy semi-final in the All Ireland).

Split Decision

Cork was the county that completely split Dublin opinion. Most of the negativity was based on the 'Real Capital' claim that Corkonians voice each and every time they speak. There was also a lot of GAA related negativity eloquently captured by the following comments:

> Their GAA teams are so far up their own arses that they think they can go on strike in an amateur sport simply because the county board wouldn't give them an extra chicken nugget in their happy meals … these guys have more chips than McDonalds.

> … the Rebel County – I'd rebel too if I came from this kip.

Cork also elicited some tear-jerkingly beautiful remarks that we've chosen not to publish as the author's opinion is that Cork heads are big enough.

Shocker

Interestingly, when the participants were asked to rank all of the counties in the order of their favourites, Dublin came in second!

Keep it in the family

Most Dubs are first generation and therefore tended to pick their parents home counties as favourites and their in-laws home counties as least favourites.

Indifference

Dubs are completely indifferent to the six northern counties with Down being the county that elicited the most indifferent opinion. Only one per cent referred to it at all under the headings of favourite and least favourite.

D'Survey

The survey was conducted using a sample population of Dubliners only. The sample consisted of all age groups ranging from fifth-class primary students (who've learned the map) at one end of the spectrum, to geriatrics who could just about remember the map at the other. The survey covered northsiders, southsiders, barmen, taxi-drivers, men, women, GAA and Leinster supporters.

CHAPTER 5

WHAT TO SEE:
A GUIDE TO THE SIGHTS
(AND THE ORDER IN WHICH
TO SEE THEM)

Curiously, if you ask Dubs what sights to see they'll usually recommend the ones that they themselves have never seen (e.g. the *Book of Kells*) or done (e.g. the Viking Splash).

While there is definitely a week's worth of sightseeing to be done in Dublin the difficulty is deciding which sights are worth seeing and which aren't.

In an attempt to address this dilemma we've categorised all of the major tourist attractions according to the type of tourist you are. For example, we've grouped all of the sights that will appeal to culture vultures under the section headed 'Sightseeing for those looking for a bit of culture' (page 65).

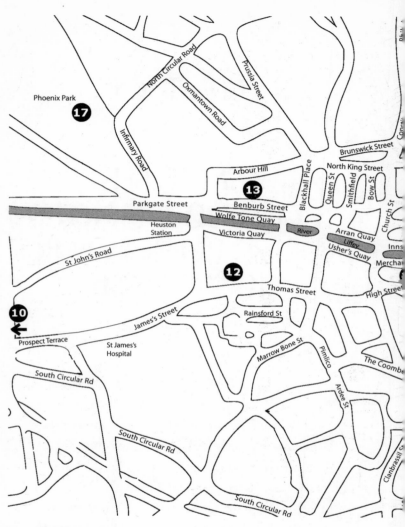

1	Molly Malone Statue	of Ireland
2	The Spire	12 Guinness Store-house
3	GPO	
4	Phil Lynott Statue	13 Collins Barracks
5	The Ha'penny Bridge	14 Bank of Ireland, College Green
6	Dublin's Doors	
7	Trinity College	
8	Dublin Castle	
9	Christ Church Cathedral	
10	Kilmainham Gaol	
11	National Gallery	

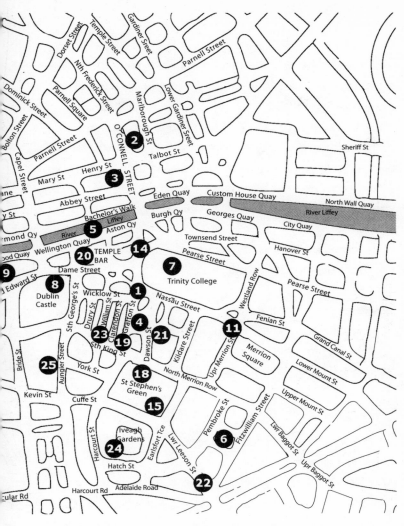

Similarly we've a section for those of you who lack a bit of culture, have kids to entertain, like to eke out the hidden treasures, etc.

Also unique to *The Culchies Guide* is our approach to recommending places to eat or drink. Rather than blandly give you a list of the restaurants and bars, we've sorted them in order of proximity to the sights that you're visiting. Where possible we've also given as blunt a review as possible.

So here are Dublin's tourist attractions sorted according to tourist personality profile:

Profile	Go see	Page
If you're the sort that is easy to impress	Molly Malone Statue	55
	The Spire	58
	Phil Lynott Statue	60
	The Ha'penny Bridge	61
	GPO	62
	Dublin's Doors	64
If you're the sort that likes a bit of culture	Trinity College	65
	Dublin Castle	67
	Christ Church Cathedral	68
	Kilmainham Gaol	70
	National Gallery of Ireland	71
	Guinness Storehouse	72
	National Museum of Ireland, Collins Barracks	73

Profile	Go See	Page
	The House of Lords, Bank of Ireland	74
If you're the sort that craves a bit of controversy	Bank of Ireland, College Green	75
If you're the sort that has kids to entertain	St Stephen's Green	78
	Phoenix Park and Dublin Zoo	78
	Dublinia and the Viking World	80
	The Viking Splash	81
If you're the sort that lacks a bit of culture	Grafton Street	82
	Temple Bar	84
	Café en Seine	85
	Ron Blacks	85
	The Sporting Emporium	85
	The Leeson Street Strip	86
If you're the sort that likes to seek out hidden treasures	The Nelson Pillar	87
	The Iveagh Gardens	88
	St Valentine's Heart	89
	Anna Livia Millennium Fountain	90
If you're in Dublin at the right time	Jan – Funderland	91
	Feb – Six Nations Rugby	92
	Mar – St Patrick's Day	93
	Apr – Colours Boat Race	94
	May – May Day Parade	94

Profile	Go See	Page
	Jun – Bloomsday	95
	Jul – Traffic	96
	Aug – Festival of World Cultures	97
	Sept – All-Ireland Finals, Croke Park	97
	Oct – Dublin City Marathon	98
	Nov – Straw Clutching at the RDS	99
	Dec – Leopardstown Races	99

SIGHTSEEING FOR THOSE THAT ARE EASY TO IMPRESS ...

In order to qualify for the 'easy to impress' section the tourist attraction has to be one that you could easily tick off your list simply by passing it in a taxi. They fit the criteria because they have no entry fee, you can't take a tour around them and most are located by the side of the road. Some of the landmarks have also qualified for this section under the 'not really a valid tourist attraction at all' rule. We'll let you figure out which ones fall into this category.

Molly Malone Statue

If you're planning your sightseeing day you need to budget about 3 minutes for this tourist gem.

Unlike most cosmopolitan cities where you'll find phoney merchandise for sale, Dublin has gone a step further and created a phoney attraction for unwitting tourists.

Now it was probably unintentional, but the whole Molly Malone legend is nothing short of farcical.

Up to 1988 Molly Malone was simply a character featured in the song 'Cockles and Mussels' – In Dublin's fair city, where the girls are so pretty, I first set my eyes on sweet Molly Malone etc., etc. However, in 1988 a statue to her memory was commissioned and the urban legend of the Tart with the Cart was born.

Also in 1988 (Dublin's millennium year) there was a press conference held in St Andrews near Grafton Street. At the conference ancient records were made public purporting that Molly Malone was in fact real and that she was baptised in St John's church in Fishamble Street sometime in the 1600s. Apparently the records reflect an entry for a Mary Malone and the powers that be were comfortable enough that this was in fact the real Molly – a Malone baptised in a church that had the word 'fish' in its street name was presumably too much to resist.

More astute researchers of the subject would argue that there were dozens of Mary Malones born in Dublin over the ages, any one of whom would have equal claim to the title.* And then there's the argument about the origins of the song itself, which has been attributed to a Scottish composer James Yorkston in the 1880s. So *if* (note the italic font) he wrote the song about one of his own experiences then presumably he based it on someone he met during his life, which would have to have been in the 1800s and not the 1600s.

Therefore, the assertion that Molly Malone ever existed doesn't stand up to a huge amount of scrutiny and the statue doesn't help. Here are some of the more notable issues with it …

---

*   Hats off to Sean Murphy, author of *The Mystery of Molly Malone*.

Her Location	Molly's statue is located at the end of Grafton Street, a site apparently influenced by its proximity to where she was baptised. Unfortunately this is research sloppiness at its best as she was baptised in St John's church in Fishamble Street. It was the press conference announcing her baptism in St John's that was held near Grafton St in St Andrew's. Confused? Now you know how they got it wrong!
Her Clothes	Molly in the statue is wearing cleavage-busting clobber of a seventeenth-century style not a nineteenth-century style.
Her Wheelbarrow	... is not a wheelbarrow it's a cart.
Her Boobs	... are huge to reflect the assertion that she was a hooker, an allegation that has no basis in fact.

All in all Molly Malone turns out to be an excellent attraction – come back in a couple of hundred years and the Dubs will probably have created more lyrical fraud and have statues of yellow submarines and the like.

And if you're peckish afterwards ...

Depending on how much you want to spend you could try (in order of damage to your wallet) O'Neills on Suffolk Street, Davy Byrnes just off Duke Street or La Cave on South Anne Street.

The Spire

New York has the Statue of Liberty, Paris has the Eiffel Tower, London has the London Eye and Dubs have 390 feet of point(lessness) stuck in the middle of the capital city.

The Spire is officially called the Monument of Light and was commissioned to replace The Nelson Pillar, which was blown up by the IRA in 1966. The pillar was originally replaced with the Anna Livia Fountain (see page 90) in 1988, but the Floozie was removed in 2001 to make way for what was to become known locally as The Spike.

And to give The Spike its due, it's not the worst bit

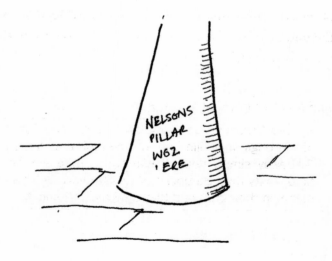

of art going and most Dubs are secretly proud of it. The things you probably won't know about The Spire are:

1. Its official birthday is 21 January 2003.
2. The steel used in its construction has been polished in a way that enhances the light reflected so that it appears different in different lighting conditions.
3. The shortlist of names from which The Spire was chosen included Dublin Sparkle, The Sword of Light and the Brian Boru Spire.
4. Dubs generally call it The Spike but it's also known as: the Stiletto in the Ghetto, the Pole in the Hole, the Pin in the Bin, the North pole, the Erection at the Intersection, the Scud in the Mud, the Rod to God and the Stiffy by the Liffey.

However, The Spire's reign as Dublin's landmark might be short-lived, as plans are already afoot to introduce another even more impressive one – a Giant Metal Man in the middle of the Liffey near the Docklands. Watch this, sorry that, space!

And if you're peckish afterwards ...

Try Leo Burdocks on Werburgh Street – the home of the original Dublin one 'n' one (fish and chips). Takeaway simply doesn't come any more authentic or tasty than Burdocks. Virtually every Dub has sampled their grub and they'd all recommend it.

Phil Lynott Statue

When it comes to Dubs, you'd have to admit that Philip Parris Lynott is one of the ones culchies would respect the most.

In case you're of a vintage that doesn't remember Thin Lizzy, Phil Lynott is the guy who wrote and performed that song you think of any time you meet someone called Saaaraah.

In brief, Phil Lynott was an iconic rock star who lived it up, rocked out and finally passed on in 1986. His statue was planted in Harry Street just steps from his favourite Grafton Street in 2005.

Despite the fact that this attraction is slotted into the easy to please category, it is in fact one of the most thoughtfully located attractions given its proximity to two fairly decent pubs (McDaids being the more salubrious of the two). If it happens to be a nice day when you're visiting grab a beer and a seat outside Bruxelles and watch true rock worshippers pay their respects to the Ace with the Bass – poignant it ain't but this is 'people watching' at its best.

You're in food heaven. Everywhere you look there's something delicious. For a simple soup and sandwich we'd go with Kehoe's on South Anne Street. For a more comprehensive menu at a reasonable price, the Café en Seine on Dawson Street. For an Asian appetite, Wagamama on South King Street. Or for an evening meal, Fire in the Mansion House on Dawson Street.

The Halfpenny or Ha'penny Bridge

This is the landmark that really epitomises Dublin and it features in most of the touristy merchandise that you'll come across. It was built in 1816 and was initially called Wellington Bridge, but its official name today is simply the Liffey Bridge.

The only *need to know* trivia is that its nickname comes from the fact that it originally had a toll of an old halfpenny. Ironically, if you do cross the bridge today you'll probably be stiffed for far more than a ha'penny by the array of homeless, harmonica-playing, *Big Issue* sellers that you'll encounter on the trip.

On the northside of the bridge you'll find one of those Dublin statues that's simply known by its colloquial name of 'the hags with the bags': you can't miss it, two bronze women chatting on a bench with their shopping bags at their feet. Of course if they were located on the other side of the bridge (the southside) they'd be known as the 'southside slags with the Prada bags'.

And if you're peckish afterwards....

You're not too far from Supermacs on O'Connell Street – go on, you know you want to.

The GPO

Most countries have a GPO but, uniquely, ours is the only one that could appear in a tourist guide under two categories:

- The *where to buy stamps* category (it's still a post office)
- The *where to see the location of the most significant armed conflict in Irish history* category

The GPO does have a tendency to make most people's list of sights to see by virtue of the latter, i.e. its association with the Easter Rising in 1916. Association is probably a slight understatement as the GPO is where most of the event took place.

The one controversial aspect to the GPO experience is the 'are they/aren't they bullet holes' conundrum. You see there are plenty of pockmarks in the stonework on the outside of the building that are supposed to be bullet holes, but a spokesperson for the GPO cleverly pointed out in a 2005 statement that the GPO had to be substantially rebuilt after the Rising; so if they are bullet holes then they're post 1916 bullet holes.

Others have commented on the fact that the holes in question are of a very neat Black & Decker quality, whereas a real bullet hole would shatter the stonework (and not drill into it). While it's plausible that these are real bullet holes, it's also plausible that they're holes left behind after the Christmas lights were taken down.

Either way, the GPO is a must for any tourist's itinerary.

And if you're peckish afterwards ...

It would be rude not to try the Gresham Hotel across the road. The Gresham opened its doors in 1817, a full year before the GPO did in 1818.

Dublin's Doors

Fitzwilliam Square is an appropriate place to have a tourist attraction because if doors actually do it for you, then you must be square.

Most of the sightseeing buses make a special stop in Fitzwilliam Square for the tourist paparazzi to snap some of the Georgian doors. Apparently Dublin is unique in having so many Georgian doors in a row – but this isn't how they've become a tourist attraction. The reason Dublin's Doors have become a tourist attraction is because they featured on an iconic poster featuring forty of Dublin's Doors. The poster itself was commissioned because there was a small collage of Dublin's Doors featured in the Irish Tourist Office in New York in the 1970s and it generated so much interest that the poster was made. Now people come to see the doors because of the poster.

Pub Grub would be the order of the day since you're surrounded by them. Apart from The Pembroke and Doheny & Nesbitts we would suggest: 1) Foley's Bar on Merrion Row just to have the Foley's Special Grill, or 2) O'Donoghues on Merrion Row for a mug of soup, a ham and cheese roll and the best pub atmosphere in the country.

SIGHTSEEING FOR THOSE LOOKING FOR A BIT OF CULTURE ...

Trinity College and the *Book of Kells*

Trinners, to the locals, is probably as cultural as Dublin gets and will hold great appeal to the 'my Gosh, to think that Samuel Beckett walked upon these very cobbles' kind of tourist. Trinity will also tick a number of boxes for the rest of us.

So what can you say about Trinity College? Well, for a start it has made it past Cornell to reach number 39 on the world college rankings; a mere 37 places behind Harvard (but catching up). Then there's the fact that it is featured in buckets of films, most notably *Educating Rrreeeettttaa* – the feel good story where an alcoholic professor (Michael Caine) tutors a Liverpudlian hairdresser (Julie Walters)

and says to her in the lecture hall 'not many people know that' for the very first time. Now there's history for you.

Of course Trinity is also home to some real life history in the form of the *Book of Kells*. Unlike its landlord, the *Book* is ranked number one in the world when it comes to examples of insular illumination (illustration) and western calligraphy. The *Book* was crafted by the world's best-fed Celtic monks about 1,200 years ago. We know this because the *Book* itself is written on vellum – which is the finest calfskin going – and it took 185 of the little guys to produce the completed manuscript. That's an awful lot of veal and it doesn't even include the calves used for the 'oops, look I've only gone and written celibate instead of celebrate – fatten up another calf there Little John ...' mistakes.

And if you're peckish afterwards ...

Try Dakota on South William Street. Non-pretentious place full of non-pretentious posers – good food and a full bar.

Dublin Castle

We're not sure about you, but we don't think a castle should be called a castle unless it has a moat going all the way around it and a huge door at the front that drops down to make a bridge.

If you're from the same school of thought as we are then you'll be disappointed that there's not a drawbridge in sight in Dublin Castle. However, it is a pretty impressive piece of work and, like all of the impressive buildings in Dublin, it was built by the British. We have done a lovely job decorating it though.

As well as its grandeur, there are two things for which Dublin Castle is best known.

Firstly, in truly cynical Irish fashion, Dublin Castle (the paragon of British rule at the turn of the century) was where the Irish Crown Jewels were stolen from in 1907 just days before King Edward VII's visit. Apparently he was none too pleased.

Secondly, Dublin Castle is situated on the very point where the Poddle and Liffey rivers meet, creating a black

pool. And it is from this black pool that Dublin (*Dubh-linn*) gets its name.

Nowadays Dublin Castle is used for big government events such as presidential inaugurations and dinner parties for visiting dignitaries. We use this building to show off Irish building skills throughout the ages, don't you know. Say nothing!

And if you're peckish afterwards ...

Try Chez Max – a French restaurant situated at the front door of the Castle – you've got to love a restaurateur who bucks the trend and doesn't go for the obvious cosy little Irish restaurant selling coddle to the thousands of tourists who pass daily. This little gem is a favourite of restaurant reviewers.

Christ Church Cathedral

Another must on the cultural tourist trail is this great big Irish Catholic church ... at least it was an Irish Catholic church until some cider-drinking Norman demolished it in 1172. We are, of course, referring to Richard de Clare (aka Strongbow), the Anglo-Norman knight and conqueror of Dublin. Yes, it was Mr Strongbow who got rid of the original Viking-built wooden church and commissioned his own stone version, which passed to the Protestant church during the reformation.

On the tour of the cathedral you can see: Strongbow's monument; the Great Nave; the Civic Pew; St Laurence O'Toole's heart; as well as plenty of other medieval history.

Tourists from Cavan and Scotland may be interested to note that you can spoof your way around the entry fee by pretending to be a worshipper and explaining this to whoever is on the cash desk (they don't charge for those actually coming to pray).

As an aside it's interesting to note that the Dublin art of nicknaming people by adding an 'o' to their name started so long ago. The fashion is obviously traceable to Strongbo' and continuing today with Anto, Bono, Jimbo, Keano etc.

And finally you may be interested to know that Strongbow, the drink, is in fact named after Strongbow, the man; and Stongbow the man got his name from his penchant for using Welsh archers during his conquests. At the time he conquered Dublin we were still using javelins. What a cheat.

And if you're peckish afterwards ...

Head straight for the Brazen Head – this is Dublin's oldest pub and dates back to 1198. It's not beyond the realms of possibility that Strongbow himself really did have a few pints of cider in this place. Anyway, no self-respecting tourist can come to Dublin without visiting the Brazen Head. Eat, drink, fall out the door.

Kilmainham Gaol

This is typically Irish – despite all the issues around over-crowding in Irish prisons we have a perfectly good one in Kilmainham that's completely empty. Mind you this one isn't of the same five-star luxury as its Mountjoy counterpart.

Kilmainham is best known for the fact that it was used to house the leaders of the 1916 Rising for a few weeks before most of them were executed. This was the catalyst for a huge swing in public opinion and the resulting War of Independence. If you do take the tour, bring some Kleenex – you'll need them.

The gaol closed its doors to new business in 1924, but has temporarily opened them again throughout the years to house such famous villains as:

Christopher Lee – playing Fu Manchu in *The Face of Fu Manchu*

Michael Caine – playing Charlie Croker in *The Italian Job*

Daniel Day-Lewis – playing Gerry Conlon in *In the Name of the Father*

Liam Neeson – playing Michael Collins in *Michael Collins*

Brian Cox – playing Frank Perry in *The Escapist*

And if you're peckish afterwards ...

Donate some cash to Paris' growing fortune and try the Dublin Hilton just up the road.

The National Gallery of Ireland

There are a number of reasons to go to the National Gallery but the principal one is that it's free.

Once you manage to negotiate your way past the hoards of Cavanmen and Scotsmen you'll be in cultural heaven: Jack B. Yeats, Rubens, Monet and Picasso are all there.

The highlight of the gallery is the painting the Jesuits had in their canteen in Dublin for sixty years that turned out to be the priceless masterpiece 'The Taking of Christ' by Caravaggio. And just in case you didn't know, you can see Caravaggio himself in the picture – he's the one carrying the lantern.

And if you're peckish afterwards ...

Don't go anywhere. While most tourist traps sell food, this place really does have a good restaurant and reputation. Since it's free in, many of the local business bods eat here at lunch.

The Guinness Storehouse

Ask anyone to name one thing that Ireland is famous for and most will say Guinness, so it's hardly surprising that the most popular tourist attraction in the city is the home of the black stuff.

The Storehouse itself used to be where the yeast was added and the final phase of the brewing process took place. Now it's a seven-storey tour and beer-drinking location for about a million tourists annually.

There's not really much we can say about Guinness that hasn't already been said. However, as far as we know, nobody has ever published the best ever Guinness practical joke before. So here it goes:

1. You'll need to order a glass of Guinness for your friend but it's absolutely essential that the glass is a straight one, i.e. if you turn it upside-down it looks the same.

2. Once the Guinness has been pulled, put a beer mat over the top, turn the glass upside-down and leave it to settle.
3. The optical illusion works a treat – as soon as they go to pick up their glass the entire contents falls on their lap and they'll never talk to you again – brilliant!

Another unpublished fact (as far as we know) is where to get the best pint of Guinness. Again we're delighted to confirm for the first time ever that the answer is Mulligans in Poolbeg Street, Dublin.

And if you're peckish afterwards …

Go to Mulligans in Poolbeg Street.

The National Museum of Ireland, Collins Barracks

Collins Barracks is home to the Decorative Arts and History segment of the National Museum.

Like most museums of its kind it exhibits all of those artefacts that were pinched, no sorry, acquired, while we were off exploring the world – chips off the old Egyptian block, etc. Mind you we weren't quite as prolific as the English in this respect who pinched, sorry acquired, whole marble walls from the likes of Greece. Our collection in this regard is modest by comparison.

The museum also houses eight galleries devoted to the military history of Ireland, that's right, eight. Obviously our Fightin' Irish reputation predates the rugby team and has some basis in history.

And if you're peckish afterwards....

Try Rhodes D7 (in the Capel Building, Mary's Abbey) – referring to none other than the spiky-haired Gary Rhodes. This place offers an understandable menu at prices that will probably surprise you (since the owner has got 5 Michelin Stars in his other places).

The House of Lords, Bank of Ireland

Bank of Ireland, College Green was originally home to the Irish parliament and it included a purpose-built House of Commons and a House of Lords. When the parliament was dissolved in 1800 the Bank of Ireland bought it and it operates as a bank today.

But the interesting thing about this building isn't the fact that the bank's cash office is in the location of the old House of Commons, nor is it the fact that you can still get a tour around the House of Lords. No sir'ee, the interesting thing about this landmark are the unclaimed items that the bank hoards in its vaults for safekeeping. This is the closest thing there is to an historic lost property department, and there's lots of it.

At the time of writing, Bank of Ireland holds property in safekeeping that some of its customers dropped in as early as the turn of the eighteenth century. And they're still waiting for someone to claim it.

SIGHTSEEING FOR THOSE LOOKING FOR A BIT OF CONTROVERSY ...

Bank of Ireland, College Green

Dublin's most controversial tourist attraction, Bank of Ireland, College Green.

Surely not.

Banks, controversy ... has to be a misprint.

This issue involves safekeeping, a service that Bank of Ireland (and indeed most banks) have provided since they opened their doors.

Now it's important that you drop the James Bond visions of safekeeping boxes that you've just conjured up in your head. Irish banks simply lumped your belongings into their own safe and left it there until you came back to claim it. And if you never come back to claim it the bank never comes looking for you. Ever! At this stage Bank of Ireland, College Green, now holds thousands of items of unclaimed property, some dating back to 1800.

So where, as a tourist, can you see these vaults? Well you can't. But if you stand outside the bank at the point where Bill Clinton addressed the nation, you're roughly standing above the vaults.

And the relevance of this? While the bank claim never to open any of this property – it really depends on who's asking. You see when Bill came to town, the American Secret Service wanted to make sure that the area above and below Bill's podium was secure so they, and their explosive-sniffing sniffer dogs, were allowed into the vaults. Apparently the bank's policy of not opening these items was quickly disregarded when the dogs raised an issue with a travel chest that had been deposited over eighty years earlier. Once opened the chest was found to contain war memorabilia including a loaded pistol.

And the controversy? Well that chest is still there

gathering dust yet it contains the most amazing and valuable memorabilia and it could belong to you!

The government gave the issue a fleeting visit at the time they drafted their dormant deposit legislation – where one Charlie McCreevy acknowledged (ironically) that the proceeds of bank robberies could be amongst the property being held in safe-keeping now by banks.

So we would encourage you to stand above these vaults as it may be the closest you'll ever get to property that you actually own – it is possible that one of your relatives dropped something in for safe-keeping and died before claiming it. And it might now be sitting in the vault below your feet. In fact if you do feel that the bank may have anything belonging to a deceased relative why not write to them – they'll love you for it. Actually they won't, but you can at least enjoy knowing that you've sent some banker off in a flap for the day!

And if you're peckish afterwards ...

Take your pick – you're in restaurant land! There does happen to be a very nice and very appropriately named joint that you might like to try – The Bank on College Green (on the opposite side of the road to the bank you've just visited). This place won the Licensing World's National Bar of the year in 2007 so if you don't enjoy it, blame them, not me.

SIGHTSEEING FOR THOSE WHO'VE GOT KIDS TO ENTERTAIN ...

St Stephen's Green

Unfortunately for parents, Dublin doesn't have any of those mega-sized Disneyland type attractions (and many would say this is a good thing). However, we do have a fair few quickies that will see you through the day.

We'd start with St Stephen's Green. For the parents there's 22 acres of gardens and statues and fountains and bandstands and pathways and memorials and archways and scenery. For the kids there are ducks.

So bring some bread, feed the ducks and move on.

And if you're peckish afterwards....

Send the kids to TGI Fridays while you go into the Shelbourne hotel for the Club Sandwich – probably the most expensive sambo in the capital but worth it.

Phoenix Park and Dublin Zoo

When you tell your kids that you're taking them to Phoenix Park you need to be able to field the obvious question, 'is there a phoenix there?' Avoid the temptation to say 'there's no such thing as a phoenix silly' and say this instead:

No sweetheart, there isn't a phoenix in the park. The park derives its name from an anglicised version of the Irish name which is Páirc an Fionn Uisce – Fionn Uisce means clear water, but it's pronounced fi-un-is-ke and sort of sounds like phoenix and that's where the name comes from. Now stop asking silly questions dopey ...

The park is completely enclosed with about 16 kilometres of walls so you could have the best game of hide and seek with your kids and not see them for days.

When you do find them there are a number of sights that you can entertain them with before taking them to the zoo. These include:

- Áras an Uachtaráin: where the president of Ireland lives
- The Papal Cross: built for Pope John Paul II's visit to Ireland, the one where he told the young people of Ireland that he loved them and didn't mention the geriatrics at all
- The Phoenix Park visitor centre: where you can enter for free and take tours, etc.

And ...

Dublin Zoo

As zoos go, Dublin Zoo is pretty good. It ticks all of the lions and tigers and bears boxes as well as boasting the whole gambit of African wildlife – elephants, zebras and co.

But the zoo's greatest export to date has been Slats, a lion born in Dublin Zoo in 1919 that was featured as the original MGM lion – the one that does the great big Rrrrrrrraaaaarrrrghhh at the start of every MGM movie. Slats appeared in all of the studios movies from 1924 to 1928.

And if you're peckish afterwards ...

Stay put and go to the Meerkat Restaurant – not exactly Michelin-starred but the kids will love the meerkats that roam freely amongst their burger and fries.

Dublinia and the Viking World

Your kids will love the fact that Dubs were originally invaded by the Vikings. Dubs themselves would have loved it if the Vikings had done a better job of the invasion so that we'd look more like the Swedes with sallow skin and blond hair. Instead the Vikings did a half job and left us with red hair and freckles.

Nonetheless, they did leave huge amounts of Viking influence and this is all captured in Dublinia – smack bang in the centre of the city where all the Vikings would have hung out in the eleventh century.

So go on, stick your kids in some Viking clobber and then chain them to the stocks while you go off for some adult cultural entertainment in Christ Church across the road.

And if you're peckish afterwards ...

See Brazen Head page 70. Alternatively try Bono's diner – the Tea Rooms at the Clarence Hotel. Not exactly a TGI Friday's type of place so the kids need to be on their best behaviour.

The Viking Splash

The kid in you will love this as much as the kids with you.

The Viking Splash is a tour around Dublin city in one of those boat/tank amphibious vehicles that you'll know from any Second World War flick – its proper title is the DUKW. You hop on the DUKW at St Stephen's Green or St Patrick's Cathedral and it takes you around all of the main city centre sights while at the same time encouraging you to scream Viking stuff at the locals as you pass – mortifying, but the kids'll love it.

To top it off you then plunge into the Grand Canal for a bit more sightseeing including U2's recording studio – Beautiful Day-ay-ay.

And if you're peckish afterwards ...

Get off at St Stephen's Green and head to BóBó's Gourmet Irish Burger joint on Wexford Street. Cows don't come any tastier than this.

SIGHTSEEING FOR THOSE THAT LACK A BIT OF CULTURE ...

Tourists in this category are driven mainly by the urge to visit a city to shop, eat and drink. In Dublin we do two of these really really well.

Grafton Street

There was a time when Grafton Street was truly unique with its Bewley's Café, Arnotts and Switzers outlets; now it could pass as any high street in any city anywhere in the United Kingdom. It's truly average.

Now its uniqueness is limited to Brown Thomas (or BT's to the locals), Weirs and the place that calls itself Bewley's but really isn't. So if you want to drop a kidney

stone on a handbag, watch or mochachino then Grafton Street is for you.

Alternatively, you could use Grafton Street as it is supposed to be used and simply pose up and down it while doing your actual shopping in any of the natty side streets. Wicklow Street, Wexford Street, the Hibernian Way and South William Street all offer decent shopping experiences, whereas the Powerscourt Townhouse Centre and Georges Street Arcade house outlets that you won't find anywhere else in the whole wide world.

And if you're peckish afterwards....

Try Saba on Clarendon Street – a Thai and Vietnamese eatery with food and atmosphere that is superior, and more than compensates for the management who simply act that way.

Temple Bar

The ideal time to visit Temple Bar would have been any time in the 1700s: a time when it would have genuinely been the centre of Dublin life. Now the best time to visit it is when it's bright. You see Temple Bar by day and Temple Bar by night are two completely different experiences.

By day it's a buzzy, vibrant, happening place to be – natty little shops, bars and restaurants.

By the time the pubs are closing Temple Bar is a testosterone, oestrogen and alcohol fuelled madhouse. The fact that local businesses got together to introduce a 'Play Nice' campaign says it all.

Despite the fact that Dublin's cultural quarter on the south bank may cater for more stag parties than we'd like, don't be put off. If you like your food, drink and shoe shops, this is the place to go.

And if you're peckish afterwards ...

Look no further than the Bad Ass Café – virtually every Dub in the 25+ age bracket has eaten something here and it is soon to exchange its Bad Ass t-shirts for a new range of Bad Ass underwear to promote its Kick Ass food. You heard it here first folks!

The Café en Seine

The Café en Seine is about as far removed from Irish culture as you can get – a ginormous pub with a French name and art deco design. But if you are in Dublin to enjoy a night out, this is the pub that would be quintessentially south County Dublin. You can therefore enjoy your night in the company of hundreds who share your indifference to Irish traditional drinking emporiums.

Ron Blacks

Another cultureless super-pub (super meaning big as opposed to superb) is Ron Blacks.

When visiting Dawson Street you have the opportunity to experience a living example of the phrase 'from the sublime to the ridiculous' by first having a drink in the original Ron Blacks – the Dawson Lounge. This is Dublin's smallest pub and it smacks of genuine Irishness. Then go and have a drink in the newer Ron Blacks. I'll let you figure out which is the sublime and which is the ridiculous.

The Sporting Emporium

Located out the back door of the Café en Seine lies another landmark devoid of any Irish culture – The Sporting Emporium. Not that there is much competition, but this is Ireland's finest casino.

Cavanmen and Scotsmen will be pleased to note that as it doesn't have a drinks' licence they give you your booze for free.

The Strip – Leeson Street

A night of non-Irish related entertainment isn't complete without a trip to the boulevard of bad dancing – Leeson Street.

Some of the nightclubs on the strip are so old it's likely that they are now playing host to second generation dancers, i.e. sons and daughters of ex-Leeson streeters are now frequenting the place. Buck Whaley's, Cats, Rios, and Leggs are all still going strong and have been complemented by Angels lap-dancing club.

SIGHTSEEING FOR THOSE THAT LIKE TO SEEK OUT HIDDEN TREASURES

The Nelson Pillar (well, parts of it!)

If you really do like to seek out the hidden history of a city then you've got to see The Nelson Pillar (or Nelson's Pillar to the locals).

The original pillar, located where the spire is now, was erected in 1808 in honour of the British Vice-Admiral Horatio Nelson. The 134-foot pillar was, however, blown up by the IRA in 1966 – so to see it in its original glory you'd need a DeLorean with a Flux Capacitor. However, in the absence of one you can still see bits of the original pillar in various locations.

The rubble went to the East Wall dump; the lettering

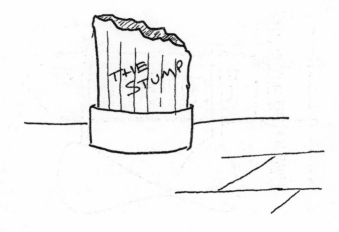

from the plinth was moved to the gardens of Butler House in Kilkenny, and Nelson's head eventually ended up in the Dublin Civic Museum in South William Street.

Nelson's Pillar was eventually replaced with The Spire in 2003. Interestingly, before The Spire became known as The Spike, Nelson's Pillar became known as The Stump. You've gotta love the Dubs penchant for naming landmarks.

And if you're peckish afterwards ...

From the Dublin Civic Museum head next-door to the Powerscourt Townhouse Centre, which offers a choice of franchise food outlets and some fairly decent restaurants.

Iveagh Gardens

Most Dubs know Stephen's Green like the back of their hand, but few are familiar with the Iveagh Gardens, which are less than 100 yards away as the crow flies.

The reason for this is that Iveagh Gardens are enclosed on most sides by offices and houses so are not in plain view. The easiest way to get in is from the Harcourt Street side (near Copper Face Jacks).

The gardens were originally part of the Guinness estate and now represent the closest thing you'll get to a *bona fide* secret garden. At the height of summer Stephen's

Green will be overflowing with visitors whereas you'd almost get away with topless sunbathing in the Iveagh Gardens.

And if you're peckish afterwards ...

If you're one of those eaters who enjoy quantity over quality you absolutely have to try the buffet lunch at the Russell Court Hotel, Harcourt Street. Relatively decent food served in enormous quantities at the most competitive prices in the city.

St Valentine's Heart

Shame on all of you who (like me) thought Valentine's Day was concocted by Hallmark.

It transpires that St Valentine was real and there is romance to his story, which in brief is:

1. He was a priest
2. He lived in Rome
3. Romans didn't like young Roman men marrying because they made bad soldiers – always wanting to return to the Mrs and not willing to die for the cause
4. Our Val let romance get the better of him so he carried out secret weddings until he was

caught, and subsequently beaten, stoned and decapitated – all in the name of love

St Valentine's heart now rests in Whitefriar Church in Aungier Street where you can join the major shareholders of Hallmark to say thanks and pay your respects.

And if you're peckish afterwards ...

An Italian would be appropriate (since he was Roman after all), so try Little Caesar's Pizza on Balfe Street. You can't go wrong.

Anna Livia Millennium Fountain

It's a little tongue in cheek to include the Anna Livia Millennium Fountain under this section but if you really, really want to seek out hidden treasures, then this one is the best hid of all.

The Anna Livia Millennium Fountain was unveiled in Dublin in 1988 to mark the city's millennium, but it was removed in 2001.

Since then she's been sitting in a crate in the council's depot in Raheny and this is where you'd have to go to see her. Alternatively you can hang on for however long it takes Dublin City Council to relocate Anna Livia to her new home at the Croppy Memorial Gardens near Collins Barracks.

The fountain itself is based on Joyce's Anna Livia

Plurabelle from *Finnegans Wake*. For those of you that missed it during its thirteen-year squat on O'Connell Street, the sculpture featured a bronze Anna doing a page three type pose in a granite waterfall, thus giving rise to various nicknames, most notably 'Viagra Falls', the 'Whore in the Sewer' and the 'Floozie in the Jacuzzi'.

SIGHTSEEING FOR THOSE WHO ARE IN DUBLIN AT THE RIGHT TIME

As with any other city, Dublin hosts many events throughout the year and there is always something happening. The most comprehensive and up-to-date site to visit is www.visitdublin.com so check that out if you're looking for something to do.

However, for the purpose of this section we really only want to identify those events that are: (a) held annually; (b) traditional-ish; and (c) held at a specific time of year.

Finding 12 was a bit of a challenge.

January

Funderland

For approximately one month every year Dublin plays host to the travelling funfair known as Funderland – the mobile equivalent to (a very small version of) Disneyland.

Funderland's annual Dublin home is in the grounds of the RDS, Ballsbridge, and you can usually spot the Ferris wheel perched outside from miles away.

So if you're the sort that likes to dose up on candyfloss and hotdogs, and then likes to be thrown about until you become nauseous, Funderland is the place for you.

February

Six Nations Rugby

There are a couple of times during the year when the Jackeen/culchie divide is forgotten and the nation unites to cheer on the national soccer, rugby or compromise rules team in Croke Park.

In February of each year the Six Nations kicks off and if you're lucky enough to be in Dublin on a home match day, you're in for a real atmospheric treat. And if the home game happens to be against the English, then you're in for either the best half-day piss-up of the year – which ends promptly at the final whistle if we're beaten – or, the best full day piss-up of the year – if we win.

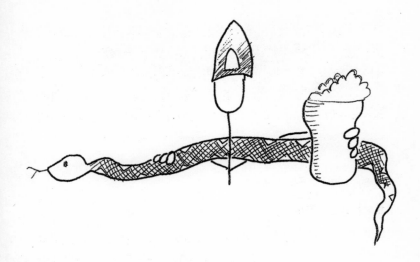

March

St Patrick's Day Parade

Dubs take the Paddy's Day parade totally for granted but when you think about it, Dublin on St Patrick's Day is up there with Time Square on New Year's Eve or Wembley on FA Cup final day. As far as the calendar of great world events goes, Dublin on 17 March is up there – unless of course you're Irish.

In the days running up to Paddy's Day the city is always buzzing with street music, comedy, céilís, night spectacles as well as the usual green pints. The festival culminates in the grand parade, which usually starts at noon and kicks off from Parnell Square.

So, if you're lucky enough to be in Dublin on 17 March and if you're turbo-charged with energy, set the alarm for an early start and head down to O'Connell Street (or any square inch of pavement close by next to a temporary barrier) and you'll be guaranteed a view which millions of people worldwide would happily grab if they'd half a chance.

April

The Colours Boat Race

Each April(ish) the boat clubs from Dublin University (the not so posh name for Trinity) and UCD square up on the Liffey to compete for the Gannon Cup by rowing up to the gates of the Guinness Brewery.

The race may not have the celebrity of the Oxford/ Cambridge equivalent but the annual Colours Boat Race has all of the rivalry (especially for UCD who are trailing a bit in the who's won the race most stakes).

The tradition is now over 60 years old and the trophy itself is a memorial perpetual cup in memory of one Ciaran Gannon – an oarsman and academic who, judging by the testimonials, was an all round good guy, and a culchie.

May

May Day Parade

It's official – unless you're a proletariat, nothing happens in Dublin in May.

For those of you with an affinity for trade unions there's the annual May Day parade. This thoroughly joyless event is held on 1 May each year and consists of a march through the city followed by ... oh who cares.

If you are in Dublin in May your best option for entertainment and atmosphere is to check out the sporting events going on elsewhere in the world and find a nice Dublin pub to watch them in. The FA Cup, the Champions League Cup final, the Heineken Cup final or even the French Tennis Open will be infinitely more enjoyable than the official events Dublin has to offer in May.

Alternatively go to www.visitdublin.com.

June

Bloomsday

A fellow scribe, James Joyce, wrote a little novel called *Ulysses*, which is based around the events of Bloomsday, 16 June 1904. (In my opinion this book is much easier to read than his!)

On the 16 June, Bloomsday is celebrated all over the world, but nowhere is it celebrated more fanatically than in Sandycove in Dublin, as this is where many of the activities in *Ulysses* take place.

So, if you do happen to be in Dublin on 16 June head to the southside where you can participate in buckets of Joycian activities including a Bloomsday breakfast in any

of the local restaurants followed by a swim in the Forty Foot (in the footsteps of Buck Mulligan from the book, who would take a dip each morning – buck-naked).

From Sandycove you can take the DART into town and have a glass of burgundy in The Duke followed by an afternoon drink in the Ormonde Quay Hotel near O'Connell Bridge (Leopold Bloom seriously liked his booze). After the Ormonde simply follow the rest of the Bloomsday brigade, who like you, will be the ones who stink of alcohol and walk funny.

July

Traffic

July is the month where there are loads of major events on everywhere except Dublin. The exodus to the music festivals alone creates so much traffic that it always makes the headlines. Our advice? www.visitdublin.com

August

Festival of World Cultures

This is a recent addition to the list of annual events in Dublin and it's good enough to knock the Dublin Horse Show into second place.

The festival takes place in Dun Laoghaire has been billed as an urban Glastonbury by some commentators. It has evolved into a three-day festival featuring food, drink, music, arts and dance from over fifty countries. This is a must for anyone who happens to be in Dublin in August.

September

All-Ireland Finals, Croke Park

Irrespective of which county (or country) you're from, you should experience Croke Park for the hurling or football finals that are held annually in September.

If you are planning a trip in September we should probably hold our hands up and dissuade you from bothering to invest in a Dublin jersey in advance of your visit to Croke Park, as the chances of Dublin featuring in one of the September finals is slim. You'll get more return on your money if you get a Kerry, Cork or Kilkenny jersey instead.

October

Dublin City Marathon

The Dublin Marathon was first run in 1980 when about 1,400 people finished it. It's now held annually in October and up to 10,000 competitors take part to run the very British distance of 26 miles, 385 yards. The urban myth is that Pheidippides ran this distance from the town of Marathon to Athens and then keeled over and died. However, the official 26.22 mile distance was first run in 1908 in the London Olympics – it started out as being roughly 25 miles but the course was lengthened to avoid some tram lines and cobbled streets.

Nowadays you can watch countless Irish men and women follow in Pheidippides' footsteps and run the marathon then keel over at the Merrion Square finish line, half dead. Within hours many will be half cut!

November

Straw Clutching at the RDS

November represents another month where there is a marked absence of any significant, uniquely Dublin events. Recently though there has been a tradition of staging some fairly decent exhibitions at the RDS in November to appeal to the Christmas shopper who may be looking for something just a little different – a helicopter or some fine art for example. These exhibitions really shouldn't qualify for a mention in this section but in the absence of anything else to report you'll have to forgive the clutching at straws!

December

The Annual Christmas National Hunt Festival, Leopardstown Races

Christmas in Dublin is probably the liveliest the city gets as the entire population does its best to attend as many parties as possible from 1 December to New Year's Eve. And as you'd expect there's buckets on including the fancy tree in O'Connell Street and de Christmus pantos at d'Olympia, Gaiety and Tivoli theatres.

But for a truly atmospheric day out simply head to

Leopardstown Racecourse where you can indulge in the two most medically and financially detrimental activities in Irish culture – drinking and gambling. You just can't go wrong.

CHAPTER 6

BELLE EIRE:
A GUIDE TO THE HOMES
OF D' RICH 'N' FAMOUS

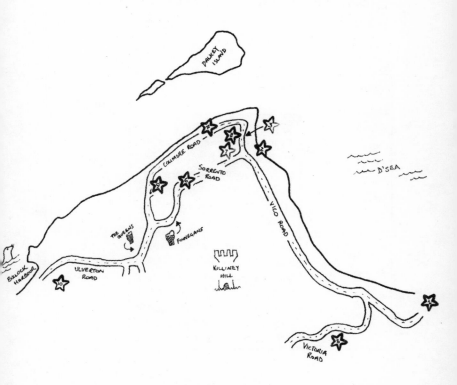

Most of the celebrities living in Dublin have chosen spots somewhere along the coast. Malahide and Howth are (or were) home to the Gay Byrne and Boyzone types, and Clontarf boasts the likes of Gerry Ryan and Joe Duffy. However, the epicentre of true A-list residency is Dalkey on Dublin's southside.

Home-grown and international consensus is that anyone who's anyone lives in Dalkey. And who could blame them? Dalkey is on the coast, jam packed with history, full of restaurants and bars and boasts the only U certificate on the Most Honest Map of Dublin Ever.

And here's who you might meet while you're there:

Who	Famous for ...	Map reference
Bono	... Leaving Ballymun as soon as he could afford to; fronting a boy band and bullying world leaders into getting fingers out of arses and changing the world – all round good guy	1
The Edge	... Dumping his real name Dave for a nickname based on his angular facial features and also for being the twenty-fourth best guitar player ever (according to Rolling Stone at least)	2

Who	Famous for ...	Map reference
Neil Jordan	... Directing the most disappointing (and to be honest, most stomach churning) strip scene in movie history – that's the *Crying Game* in case you missed it	3
Jim Sheridan	... Movie writing and producing and for making Daniel Day-Lewis very rich and very famous	4

Who	Famous for ...	Map reference
Enya	... Singing about wanting to sail away, sail away, sail away	5
Maeve Binchy	... Writing and writing and writing and writing and writing and still going	6
Eddie Irvine	... Rear-ending Michael Schumacher (and countless others)	7
Van Morrison	... Being the man	8
Chris De Burgh	... Sleeping with Miss World's mother and grandmother – no, sorry, nanny	9
Gerard Charlton	... Suing some guy called Pat Kenny for squatting on his land	10

Note:

There is a certain etiquette that locals tend to adopt when they come into contact with a celeb and that is to pretend that they: (a) haven't seen them at all; (b) have no idea who they are; or (c) know exactly who they are but treat them merely as neighbours – a casual 'howya Bono' type of interaction.

This means that the celebs enjoy a certain anonymity in their locality. So when visiting you can: (a) act like a local and ignore them; or (b) turn into a member of the paparazzi by taking sneaky pictures, asking for autographs and stealing memorabilia at all possible opportunities.

Please go for (b). Thanks.

But it's no coincidence that so many A-listers have congregated in the same place – Dalkey is one of Dublin's most picturesque, historic and fashionable towns and here's what it has to offer:

Sightseeing

Killiney (or Dalkey) Hill	A public park opened in 1887 to celebrate Queen Vic's fiftieth year on the throne (some bout of constipation that must have been).
Dalkey Heritage Centre	The centre includes a fifteenth-century medieval townhouse and a tenth-century graveyard, if you're into that sort of thing
Coliemore Harbour	The original Dublin port
Dalkey Island	An island with tons of rabbits, goats, birds, seals, a couple of ruins and a brilliant view into the back gardens of the residents of Coliemore Road
Vico Road	A panoramic view of Dublin bay that represents Ireland's answer to the Bay of Naples (and gives it a fairly good run for its money)

Drinking

The Queens	Original home of RTÉ's *The Restaurant* don't you know! But also home to Dalkey's best beer garden. If you're planning to visit go on a Saturday, as this is when the locals bring out their mid-life crises for a spin. You can enjoy a beer whilst watching some serious hardware pass by
Finnegan's	Arguably the best pub in Dalkey and definitely the pub with the most affluent clientele in the country. Everyone from Mel Gibson to Salmon Rushdie** has boozed here
The Club	There are a total of six bars in Dalkey but if you're stuck for time and have to limit your pub crawl to three venues, The Club should make your shortlist

Eating

Don Giovanni	The least arsey of the Italian restaurants in Dalkey
Ragazzi	The most arsey Italian restaurant in Dalkey, but it is the choice of most A-listers. Worth a visit if only to see the graffiti in the place
Jaipur	The subject of the most kiss-ass review this author has ever seen but apparently they deserved it

---

**   Finder's fee to Jim Connolly, cheers

Guinea Pig	If you're looking for something a little more intimate and prepared to pay the price
The Queens	Most commercially orientated restaurant, so they'll have something to tickle most fancies
Borza	Decent take-away that's been clogging up the arteries of locals and tourists alike for decades

CHAPTER 7

A CULCHIE'S SURVIVAL GUIDE

Dublin may be big in comparison to your home town, but as far as cities go it's easy to figure out. The same can be said of Dubs themselves. While there are many headings under which you and dubs differ, these differences are easy to identify. Once you know what they are you'll be better able to understand how Dubs work.

Cultural Differences

First Impressions

Dubs tend to think of you as innocent and gormless, but likeable all the same. They base this opinion on the fact that if you had any sense you would never live in the country, you'd live in Dublin. Those of you that do go to Dublin are therefore elevated in the mind of the Dub. After no time you'll become fully accepted and this will become apparent when you notice that Dubs will demean other culchies to your face (they now see you as a peer).

In advance of being fully accepted you'll notice two things about Dubs straight away:

- They have no idea where anywhere outside Dublin is.
- They have a definite superiority complex that manifests itself in the need to demean your town – 'Kilty-bleedin' wha? Jaysus the best thing outta that place is the Dublin Road, wha' (Dub proceeds to fall over in laughter).

TV Privileges

Another thing you need to bear in mind when talking to a Dub is the fact that they have grown up with access to BBC, UTV and Channel 4 since the early 1980s, whereas most of the rest of the country were lucky to get a fuzz free RTÉ signal up until recently. This difference manifests itself as persistent references to people and events you've never even heard of – Noel Edmonds' *Swap Shop*, Mike Reeds *Runaround*, Roy Castle's *Record Breakers*, Trevor

Jordash, Anna Friel's lesbian kiss, *The Young Ones*, *The Tube*. There's no denying that Dubs have led a privileged TV life.

Independence

Other noticeable Dublin characteristics include the fact that life in Dublin seems to operate at a slightly faster pace than in the rest of the country. Dubs always appear to walk at a speed that suggests they're late – give it a few more years and they'll morph into New Yorkers.

But despite their savvy, busy, busy, VIP appearance, Dubs are the least independent specimens in the country.

Whereas most of the rest of the country have left home by the time they're eighteen to work or go to college or whatever, Dubs have all these amenities on their doorstep, making leaving home unnecessary – so they don't. And because they don't your average Dub can't cook, clean or cope on their own. Therefore, a huge percentage of Dubs don't leave home until they've replaced their mums with a husband or wife.

GAA

Dubs love their GAA but their love isn't nearly as deep as the love the rest of the country has for their teams.

For example:
- Dubs would rarely be able to name the full team, whereas a Kerryman or woman would name the team, the subs and the selectors.
- Dubs never travel to matches – ever.
- Dubs show little respect for the opposition – despite the fact that they live in Dublin, Dub supporters are inevitably late for home games and are often the cause of matches being delayed.
- Dubs can be intimidating, especially in Hill 16 and very especially when they're losing. Mind you, the Hill is one of those experiences you won't forget in a hurry: the banter is robust; the smell of booze is as strong as the smell of drugs; and occasionally you'll hear

THE ONLY ALL IRELAND
HURLING TROPHY INVOLVING
A DUB !

something that'll make you fart with fear – 'Wachu
lookin at muck savage? I'll bleedin' do time for you'–
sort of stuff.

- Dubs know less about hurling than they do about
football.

In relation to the last point, you may want to file away the
following bit of trivia for your next GAA debate with a
Dub:

FACT

Dublin has won the Senior All-Ireland hurling title on six

separate occasions, the last one in 1938. BUT in all of those teams there was in fact only one Dublin-born player and that was Jim Byrne from the 1938 team; the rest were culchies. Ouch!

Living in Dublin

There are four areas of Dublin that most culchies tend to gravitate towards and these are:

Rathmines
Ranelagh
Portobello
Phibsborough

Not surprisingly these areas also coincide with the location of many colleges. The interesting point to note is that culchies continue to live in these areas long after graduation. This is probably because culchies tend to socialise in particular pubs and clubs, the majority of which are located near or in Rathmines, Ranelagh, Portobello and Phibsborough. And these are:

Copper Face Jacks, Harcourt Street

This place is the true epicentre of culchie socialising. It's not only renowned for the rural nature of its clientele, but also specifically for the concentration of nurses and guards that frequent the place. It also has a local, national and international reputation as a cattle mart. Apparently if you can't score in this place you might as well give up.

Rody Bolands, Rathmines

In the words of one internet pub-feedback contributor Rody's is ... the absolute best pub in the world. Barstaff,

DJ's and bouncers are all very friendly and some even quite cute. Music is fantastic and the atmosphere even better ... best bit is it's full of culchies. Need we say more?

Flannerys, Camden Street

Owned, bounced, run and frequented by culchies. Everything you'd want from a pub – from quiz night on a Monday to big screen GAA matches on a Sunday, all in the company of your rural brethren. Fantastic.

McGowans, Phibsborough

This is where you'll find the largest concentration of drunken culchies on the northside.

The Portobello, South Richmond Street

Where the rural residents of Portobello drink, dance (in Rain NiteClub) and pull.

CHAPTER 8

DUBLINGO: A GLOSSARY OF DUBLIN SLANG, RHYMING SLANG, PHRASEOLOGY AND VOCAB

Just so's you know ...

Dubliners have developed their own rhyming slang but to understand it completely you need to rhyme the slang with how Dubs would pronounce it. For example, a Joanna is rhyming slang for a piano or 'pee-anna' as a Dub would pronounce it. I've included many of the most frequently used ones below:

Arthur Scargle *n.* rhyming slang meaning gargle or drink.

Banjaxed *adj.* colloquial reference meaning: (1) broken, e.g.
   'You must've been doin' over fifty cus the exhaust on the

Cinquecento is banjaxed'; (2) hung-over, e.g. '*Never touching that Blue Nun shite again – I'm banjaxed*'.

Barry *n*. shortened from Barry White, rhyming slang for a toilet-based activity that rhymes with White, e.g. '*That curry's playing havoc with the plumbing, I'm off for a Barry*'. ▶ Gladys *n*.; Pony *n*.

Blem *v*. usually used in reference to the act of kicking a football really, really hard, e.g. '*He burst it, he blemmed it so hard*'.

Boat race *n*. rhyming slang for face ▶ Brendan Grace *n*.

Bollix /bol-icks/ *n*. meaning testicles, e.g. '*She had me by the bollix*'.

Dogs-bollix *n*. reference to something of high quality, e.g. '*Houghton's chip was the dogs bollix*'.

Bonce *n*. colloquial reference meaning head, e.g. '*Jaysus, couldn't believe the bleedin' judge would believe a guard over me, he was wrekin' me bonce*'.

Brasser /bra-zer/ *n*. (pl. Brassers) a prostitute.

Brassers /bra-sirs/ *adj*. reference to cold weather, e.g. '*Jaysus it's brassers, I'll be pissin ice cubes*'. (Origin – shortened from the phrase 'to freeze the balls off a brass monkey' referring to the brass mount used to hold cannon balls in a pyramid structure – cold weather caused the brass monkey to contract thus making the cannon balls dismount.)

Brendan Grace *n*. rhyming slang for face ▶ Boat race *n*.

Brown Bread *adj*. classic rhyming slang meaning dead and used most appropriately by one of the tabloids in a headline to mark the death of Pat Higgins (the original Pat the Baker) in 2007. The headline simply read '*Pat the Baker – Brown Bread*'.

Buck Shee *adj*. rhyming slang meaning free.

Chisler /chiz-e-ler/ *n*. (pl. chislers) colloquial reference to a child ▶ God-forbids *n*.

Creamed *adj*. shortened from cream krackered – rhyming slang for knackered meaning tired.

Culchie /kul-shee/ *n*. (pl. culchies) a term used to describe a person from rural Ireland (poss. origins: (1) from Gaelic *cul an tí* meaning back of the house; (2) from *coilte-mach* the Gaelic translation of Kiltimagh, County Mayo; (3) English abbr. of Agricultural Science which was introduced as a degree in UCD in the 1960s – agricultural being shortened to culchie and adopted to mean rural students) ▶Mucker *n*.; Bogger *n*.; Redneck *n*.; Mulchie *n*.; Country bumpkin *n*.; Muck Savage *n*.

Daniel Day *n*. rhyming slang and word play referring to Daniel Day-Lewis – a play on the word for the Dublin tram the Luas (pronounced Lewis) ▶ Jerry Lee *n*.

Gas Cooker /gas kew-ker/ *n*. rhyming slang for snooker or snew-ker to a Dub.

Gladys *n*. shortened from Gladys Knight, rhyming slang for a toilet-based activity that rhymes with Knight ▶ Barry *n*.; Pony *n*.

God-forbids *n*. rhyming slang meaning kids. ▶ Chisler *n*.

Gushie /guh-shee/ *v.* the activity of throwing an item between two or more individuals competing to retrieve it.

Harrys *n.* Dublin demi-rhyming slang. The correct slang term is Harry Rags referring to fags or cigarettes.

Hit 'n miss *n.* rhyming slang meaning piss ▶ Jimmy.

Jackeen *n.* (pl. Jackeens) a subtly derogatory term used to describe someone from Dublin, Ireland (poss. origin: shortened from Union Jack – jack being suffixed by the Gaelic for small 'ín', but pronounced 'een' to produce Jackeen and taken to mean 'little Brit'). ▶ Dub *n.*

Jammer *n.* shortened from *jam-jar* – rhyming slang for a car.

Jays fluid /j's flewed/ *n.* rhyming slang for nude or new'ed in Dub speak.

Jerry-Lee *n.* /jer-ee-lee/ rhyming slang and word play referring to Jerry Lee Lewis – a play on the word for the Dublin tram the Luas (pronounced Lewis) ▶ Daniel Day *n.*

Jimmy *v.* shortened from jimmy riddle – rhyming slang for piddle, i.e. to urinate ▶ Hit 'n miss *v.*

Joanna *n.* rhyming slang for a piano or a *pee-annah* in Dub speak.

Jockey *n.* generally refers to a rider of a horse but is used colloquially in Dublin in reference to a male lover, e.g. '*Anto is Jacinta's jockey*'.

King Lears *n.* rhyming slang for ears.

Malahide *n*. Dublin rhyming slang meaning ride, which itself is a colloquial reference to: (1) *n*. a beautiful person (with whom you would like to have …); (2) *v*. intercourse.

Mince pies *n*. rhyming slang for eyes.

Miwadi *n*. rhyming slang meaning body.

Moxy *adj*. colloquial reference meaning horrible, usually used in reference to human characteristic, e.g. '*ya moxy bollix ya*'.

Muck Savage *n*. derogatory term for a Mucker, sorry a Red Neck, no sorry a sheep-shagger, no rather a person from rural Ireland ▶ Culchie.

Nads *n*. an abbreviated reference to gonads meaning testicles or balls, e.g. '*… and then she kicked me straight in the nads*'. ▶ Bollix.

Nat *n*. shortened from Nat King Cole, rhyming slang meaning hole, which itself refers to: (1) one's backside, e.g. '*… work gives me a pain in me Nat*'; (2) intercourse, e.g. '*… it's been so long since I got me nat that it's got cobwebs on it now*' ▶ Swiss *n*.

Ned *n*. shortened from Ned Kelly, rhyming slang for belly.

One 'n one *phrase* colloquial reference to one fish 'n one chips.

Ones 'n twos *n*. rhyming slang meaning shoes.

Pale *adj*. a stake marking a boundary. Dublin Pale refers to the area of Dublin that was subject to British influence, which is last recorded as a twenty mile radius around the city.

Pony *n.* shortened from Pony and Trap meaning crap ▶ Barry *n.*; Gladys *n.*

Redneck *n.* derogatory term for a person from rural Ireland (origin: (1) reference to the sunburn mark around every muckers neck; (2) the mark a culchies mother leaves whilst slapping them on the back of the neck telling them to get up to Dublin and get a job) ▶ Mucker *n.*; Bogger *n.*; Culchie *n.*; Mulchie *n.*; Country bumpkin *n.*; Muck Savage *n.*

Roasters *n.* shortened from roast joint (pronounced *joynt*), rhyming slang for pint (or *point*).

Seamus Heaney *n.* rhyming slang for a bikini.

Skin Diver *n.* rhyming slang for fiver referring to five euro.

Swiss *n.* shortened from Swiss roll meaning hole, which itself refers to: (1) one's backside, e.g. '... *she'd give you a pain in the Swiss*'; (2) intercourse, e.g. '... *so, you bought the Bacardi breezers so I presume you got your Swiss?*' ▶ Nat *n.*

Tennis racket *n.* rhyming slang meaning jacket.

Tin *n.* shortened from tin of fruit, rhyming slang meaning suit.

Tobler /tow-blur/ *adj.* Dublin demi-rhyming slang meaning own as in on your tobler, on your own. (origin: shortened from the word 'Toblerone').

Top notch *adj.* colloquial reference meaning the best, e.g. '*the thruppenies on yer one were top notch*'.

ACKNOWLEDGEMENTS

Of all the people that contributed to this book very few deserve an acknowledgement but most of them asked 'am I getting a mention'. So Gary, Steve, Joe, Dave, James, Padraig, Niall, Andrew, Eoin, Bren, John, Maura, Mags and Elaine, the answer to that is *No*.

On the other hand, Jackeens – Denis 'the Squire' Houton, Dave 'Erindipity' Kenny, Ross 'Wagamama' Cregan, Philip 'Kilimanjaro' Brady and Kev 'Lovely Bit of Biz' Lyons did contribute their humour, prejudiced opinions and colourful vocab, so thanks lads (Pint, pint, pint, pint, pint, pint – the pints I owe you).

However, those that deserve the most thanks are the rural folk who vented all of their Dublin issues in a manner that must have felt like therapy for them. There are almost too many to mention but amongst them are (in order of their culchieness) Johnny Mc, all of the Manorhamilton cousins, Donough, Kerry Gill, Cork Gill, and Big John C.

As always there wouldn't be a book if there wasn't a willing and able publisher so a huge thanks to Eoin, Wendy the rest of the team at Mercier who (despite their stubbornness over titles) are not only willing and able, but are also fantastic to work with.

And finally, whilst thanks to all my family goes without saying, a few have to be singled out as they light up my life and make Dublin a utopia for me – of course they are Jo, Ally, Shaunie and King Bobby.

P.S. Sorry Laura-Kate, Keelin, Steph, Carrie, Aaron and Ava – maybe you'll get a mention in the next book!

INDEX